WELCOME TO THE WORLD OF
Frogs and Toads

Diane Swanson

WALRUS
B O O K S

Copyright © 2002 by Diane Swanson
Walrus Books, an imprint of Whitecap Books
3rd printing, 2012

Visit our website at www.whitecap.ca.

The information in this book is true and complete to the
best of the author's knowledge. All recommendations
are made without guarantee on the part of the author or
Whitecap Books Ltd. The author and publisher disclaim
any liability in connection with the use of this information.

Edited by Elizabeth McLean
Cover design by Steve Penner
Interior design by Margaret Ng
    Typeset by Jacqui Thomas and Jane Lightle
Photo research by Tanya Lloyd Kyi
Cover photograph by John Mielcarek/Dembinsky
    Photo Assoc
Photo credits: Skip Moody/Dembinsky Photo Assoc iv, 2,
    18; Rob and Ann Simpson 4; John Mielcarek/Dembin-
    sky Photo Assoc 6, 12, 16; Kitchin & Hurst 8, 10; Gary
    Meszaros/Dembinsky Photo Assoc 14; Jens Vindum/Cal-
    ifornia Academy of Sciences 20; Photo on 22 courtesy of
    ACO Polymer Products, Inc.; Wayne Lynch 24, 26

Printed and bound in Canada

Library and Archives Canada Cataloguing in Publication

Swanson, Diane, 1944–
    Welcome to the world of frogs and toads

Includes index.
ISBN 1-55285-354-3
ISBN 978-1-55285-354-2

    1. Frogs—North America—Juvenile literature. 2.
Toads—North America—Juvenile literature. I. Title.

QL668.E2S92 2002   j597.8'097   C2002-910806-3

The publisher acknowledges the financial support of the
Canada Council for the Arts, the British Columbia Arts
Council, and the Government of Canada through the Canada Book Fund (CBF). Whitecap Books also acknowledges
the financial support of the Province of British Columbia
through the Book Publishing Tax Credit.

Canada Council   Conseil des Arts
for the Arts   du Canada

BRITISH COLUMBIA
ARTS COUNCIL

ENVIRONMENTAL BENEFITS STATEMENT

Whitecap Books Ltd saved the following resources
by printing the pages of this book on chlorine free
paper made with 10% post-consumer waste.

WATER	SOLID WASTE	GREENHOUSE GASES
90	6	20
GALLONS	POUNDS	POUNDS

Environmental impact estimates were made using the Environmental Paper Network
Paper Calculator. For more information visit www.papercalculator.org.

Contents

World of Difference

WARTY OR SMOOTH. DRY OR MOIST. There's little real difference between the croaking critters folks call "toads" and those called "frogs." Many warty, dry-skinned croakers have toady names. But to scientists, they're just frogs that have adapted to different kinds of homes.

Frogs and toads are all amphibians: animals that spend part of their lives in water and part on land. While other amphibians—such as salamanders and newts—have tails, adult frogs and toads do not.

There are about 3500 kinds of frogs and toads in the world, but they don't all live in

Like other frogs and toads, the American toad oozes toxins from its skin.

1

A gray tree frog blends well with the fungus it sits on.

North America. Canada and the United States are home to about 100 different kinds. With its warmer climate, Mexico has even more.

The grass frog is one of the smallest in North America—and the world. It's only the size of your thumbnail. At the other extreme are bullfrogs that can measure 20 centimetres (8 inches) from end to end.

Frogs and toads come in several colors, including brown, black, green, yellow, and white. Many can hide by blending in with what's around them. A brown tree frog called a spring peeper, for example, is hard to spot among dead leaves.

Shifts in light, moisture, and temperature can cause frogs and toads to vary their colors. A little Pacific tree frog might change from green to gray to yellow and back to green again—all within eight minutes.

FABULOUS FROGS, TERRIFIC TOADS

As common as they are, frogs and toads still amaze people. Here are some of the reasons why:

- Just by sitting on damp soil, a spadefoot toad can absorb water through its skin.
- Lightweight tree frogs can walk upside down—even on smooth surfaces.
- Over the summer, a single toad can eat as many as 10,000 insects.
- Sucked up by hurricanes, little frogs sometimes travel long distances before falling like rain.

3

Where in the World

IN THE GRASS, BENEATH A ROCK, UNDER THE WATER, UP A TREE. Frogs and toads are almost everywhere and on every continent, except Antarctica. Most are found in hot, humid countries, but wood frogs live farther north than the Arctic Circle!

Different kinds of frogs and toads adopt different kinds of homes, including damp forests, dry deserts, cold mountain streams, and city gardens. Some spend much of their time in water. Others live mostly on land—even underground—or up in trees and bushes.

A good burrower, this spadefoot toad peeks out of its little hole.

5

The large eardrum behind the eye of the bullfrog is easy to spot.

Body temperatures of frogs and toads change with their surroundings. Some dig burrows or bury themselves in sand or mud to cool down and avoid drying out. In Mexico and southern Texas, the Mexican burrowing toad spends a lot of its life beneath the surface. Like most tunneling frogs and toads, it digs in backward, scraping and scooping with knobs on its hind feet.

In places with cold winters, many frogs bury themselves in the bottom of ponds and small lakes. They live on fat stored in their bodies and take in oxygen from the water through their skin. They sleep deeply—hibernate—for months.

Day to day, frogs and toads don't usually travel far. Many hunt for food inside their own territories. Then they head back to shelter, often settling under stones and logs.

Capture frogs and toads from one pond, and release them in another? BAD idea! Adding new kinds of frogs and toads to any pond causes trouble.

Big bullfrogs from eastern North America were taken to many parts of western North America and raised as food for people. When these aliens moved into an area, they soon spread out on their own. The bullfrogs have been eating up small western frogs, such as red-legged frogs, as well as fish, snakes, and birds.

World in Motion

HAVING NO TAIL HELPS FROGS AND TOADS JUMP. That makes it easier for them to kick off with both back legs at the same time. Frogs and toads with narrow bodies and long legs usually leap the farthest. Those with wide bodies and short legs often just hop or walk.

In water, the animals can swim fast by kicking their back legs much as they do when they're jumping on land. They spread out their webbed back feet to push their bodies forward, and they press their front legs tightly against their sides.

Instead of swimming, warty northern

Up, off, and away! A bullfrog makes a mighty leap.

9

It's easy for a Pacific tree frog to squat safely on a skinny stem.

cricket frogs and a few others sometimes skip across a pond. With a series of quick jumps, they can bounce along the surface.

Little tree frogs get around mostly by climbing—grabbing onto twigs or branches. To escape danger from enemies such as snakes and birds, they usually jump. And they're good at it! Large sticky pads on their toes help them hang onto almost everything. Some also have a sticky webbing between their toes. These frogs can cling to surfaces as steep and smooth as windows and doors.

Balancing on slender twigs is no problem for tree frogs. Their slightly flattened bodies make it possible for them to spread their weight out evenly. They also press their loose belly skin snugly against any surface, which helps to hold them in place.

Ready, set...leap. Every year, there's a special track and field event—the Jumping Frog Jubilee—held in Angels Camp, California. To enter, frogs must be at least 10 centimetres (4 inches) long. Each one makes three jumps, then judges measure the total straight-line distance to its final landing spot.

A champion bullfrog, named Rosie the Ribiter, holds the unbroken record. In 1986, she covered a distance greater than the length of three beds placed end to end.

World Full of Food

FLIES, ANTS, SLUGS, AND WORMS—
all yummy meals for frogs and toads! They
dine on what's handy and small enough to
fit into their mouths. Big croakers also feast
on mice, small snakes, fish—even other
frogs and toads. Some also catch bats that
swoop to the water at night to drink.

It's lucky that frogs and toads aren't fussy
eaters. Stuck in a basement or garage, toads
easily change their menu from worms and
butterflies to spiders and centipedes.

Frogs that spend much of their lives in
water can hide and hunt at the same time.
Their big eyes and nostrils usually sit on the

Thick, green
duckweed makes
a great cover
for a hungry
green frog.

Chomp! A leopard frog captures a dragonfly for lunch.

tops of their heads, so the frogs can see and breathe while keeping mostly out of sight. There's a hitch, though. The frogs can't spot what's right in front of their noses. For that, they have to turn sideways.

A long tricky tongue serves most frogs and toads well. It's normally attached to the front of the mouth, so it can zoom out far to catch dinner. The food sticks to the gooey tip and is drawn in as the tongue returns to the mouth. The whole operation is very fast. One high-speed camera filmed a toad's tongue as it shot out, nabbed a worm, and returned—all in less than .07 second.

Catching food is harder work for the tailed frog of North America's mountain streams. Its tongue is attached to the back—not the front—of its mouth, so the frog has to catch insects by snapping them up.

Now you see it. Now you don't. Whatever frogs and toads catch for lunch is normally swallowed whole. To get the food down, a meal might take two or three gulps—plus some help from the critter's eyeballs.

Muscles pull on one or both of the eyes, pressing them down hard against the roof of the mouth. That forces the food back and into the animal's throat. No wonder frogs and toads blink wildly as they swallow.

World of Words

MOST FROGS AND TOADS ARE BUILT TO SING. Besides their strong voice boxes, large stretchy vocal sacs help them make sounds. The singing ranges from warbles to whistles and croaks to chuckles. Some of the songs are short, while others can last for several minutes.

Each kind of frog and toad makes its own special type of music. Cricket frogs click. Chorus frogs rattle. Mexican tree frogs sputter. Wood frogs quack. The smaller animals usually produce high-pitched tones, while large ones often have deep-pitched voices. But when it comes to volume, even

A singing spring peeper inflates its see-through vocal sac.

little frogs and toads can make a lot of noise. The shrill singing of a spring peeper can be heard 800 metres (about half a mile) away—and sometimes all night long!

Many kinds of male frogs and toads sing to attract mates at breeding times. They crowd together and croon. The females depend on these songs—more than sight or smell—to find males to mate with.

When it's time to mate, green frogs gather together.

18

Male frogs and toads might sing to warn other males to go away. The singing also interrupts the mating songs of their competition.

Grabbed by an enemy, such as a hungry heron or raccoon, frogs and toads might scream. The noise doesn't act as a warning to others, but it can shock the enemy into letting its victim go. Still, there are moments when it's best to say nothing and simply play dead. Animals hunting for live food ignore these frogs and toads.

SORTING THE SONGS

It was a warm spring night as a female bullfrog arrived at the edge of a pond. The voices of many different frogs and toads were already filling the air. Green frogs were plinking and plunking. Spring peepers were whistling, and American toads were trilling for 10 seconds at a time.

The bullfrog waited, listening closely for just one song. Suddenly, she heard "Jug o'rum. Jug o'rum." And with that, she was off to find the singer—a mate for herself.

World of Mates

The tailed frog has no true tail, but its tail-like part helps it mate.

WATER IS WHERE MATING FROGS AND TOADS OFTEN HEAD. They gather by the hundreds—or thousands—at ponds, shallow lakes, swamps, drainage ditches, even puddles. Some find their way to the same spot year after year, using smells, sights, and sounds to guide them.

Changes in light, temperature, and moisture help signal the start of breeding seasons. And for many frogs and toads, that means springtime. The seasons are long for some kinds, short for others. Bullfrogs, for instance, have several months each year to meet and mate, while wood frogs in the

For small animals, using a "toad tunnel" is the safest way to cross a road.

north might have only a day or two.

Female frogs and toads often respond to the songs of the males, who usually call out from good egg-laying places. But some males sit in silence. Then they try to grab females as they head toward the singing males.

Oddly, male tailed frogs have no voices at all. They have to find their mates by swimming silently over river-beds. Male western toads can produce sounds, but they can't all make breeding calls. Instead, they might hunt for mates day and night, grabbing whatever seems like a female toad—even a thick twig in the water.

When most frogs and toads mate, the male grasps the female tightly with his front legs. As soon as she lays her eggs, he fertilizes them. If a male clutches a female who has already released her eggs, she makes a special sound that tells him she has mated.

TOAD TUNNELS

Toads crossing busy highways to reach mating ponds risk getting killed. Many travel in such large groups that a single car can strike down dozens at a time.

People in parts of North America created tunnels beneath some high-traffic roads along toad routes. They built low fences to guide the critters toward the entrances. The tunnels work so well that they've almost completely wiped out toad road deaths in their areas.

New World

EGGS IN CLUMPS. EGGS IN STRINGS. And a few frogs lay their eggs in foam. By kicking their legs, white-lipped frogs in Texas and Mexico whip mucus and water into a stiff froth, or foam. This bubbly "nest" protects the eggs from getting too hot or drying out.

Depending on which kinds of frogs or toads they are, the females might lay only a few eggs or several thousands! Hatching times also vary, but one day, young frogs and toads—called tadpoles—emerge from the eggs. They seldom look anything like their parents. They don't even have legs.

Wood frog tadpoles will hatch out of this clump of eggs.

A muddy puddle can be home to spadefoot toad tadpoles.

Instead, the tadpoles have long, strong tails that help them swim. Like fish, they breathe with gills, not lungs.

Hungry tadpoles eat just about any plants and bacteria they can. They might also dine on animals that have died in the water. For feeding in swift streams, tailed frog tadpoles have big suckers that help them stay in place.

As tadpoles grow, their bodies change. Their tails and gills disappear, and they develop legs and lungs. They begin to look like adult frogs and toads, and soon they're ready to leave the water. Many kinds of tadpoles become adults a few months after they hatch. Some kinds take only days, while others take years.

Throughout their lives, toads and frogs struggle to escape enemies, such as newts, crows, and skunks. They don't usually live long, but bullfrogs might possibly turn 15 or 20.

TADPOLE-EATING TADPOLES

Spadefoot toad tadpoles that often hatch in rain puddles sometimes feed on their brothers and sisters! Although most of these tadpoles gobble up bits of plants in the water, others become meat-eaters.

The tadpoles grow quickly— but not always quickly enough. If a puddle is drying up faster than the plant-eaters are maturing, the meat-eating tadpoles devour them, developing even more rapidly. It's all just a matter of survival!

Index